The Economy of the Celestial Empire: Poems

by Don Brandis

Robin Hood and Maid Marion on Leaving Sherwood Forest to Become Realtors

a day recovers what the night had claimed

a brisk walk inventories neighborhoods

that alternating kingdoms can't retain

thistle, hawthorn signal understood
for having been each morning re-explained
mornings recover what the night reclaimed

do what you want, not what we knew you would
the only motives; only one's displayed
our alternating kingdoms can't sustain

a raging discontent remakes the world
it's brightened image barely masks its pain
the day recovers what the night won't claim

acceptance with a heart of oak withstood
what passed for evil now will pass for good
through alternating kingdoms unsustained

your day's sometimes my night. I can't complain
another choice awaits another name
what alternating kingdoms can't explain

one day accepts as night at last renamed

Visiting the Skagit

Broad, flat. Even cultivated the Skagit is river-made
strip malls creep north along the Interstate
and in fifty years will bury its hearty fields

a dozen cows stand in a corner of pasture
re-chewing old dinners; the effort to lean down
and feed tiresome and one stomach's already bloating.

A wide patch of snow geese have settled nearby
with others circling lazily overhead
those on the ground pick at scraps of grain

a late plowing has scattered
among clumps of coal-colored mud
perhaps to lure them.

A fair November day of colored leaves
now mostly grounded, the few left hanging
flutter alone, no longer low-clattering
against each other like shuffled cards.

Tunnels open silently in the landscape
triggered by location sentinels like boulders
left behind by receding glaciers

or extinct animals long buried in the Burgess Shale
whose distorted remains we ponder
trying to guess their living contours

tunnels of Memory darkened now but for shards of light
glittering, sharp enough to attract a glance
a rusty fish hook bit reflexively by a passing thought

Intentions are the final mystery
we find ourselves moving before deciding to
as we are constant motion and desire

with or without awareness whose mirrorings
each arising superfluous, contingent, random
until becoming past and therefore necessary.

Did we come to be reminded
of what lies frozen in forms like Stonehenge
a calculator/predictor of solar eclipses?

the sun mounting, the moon receiving
and for no-time there is nothing, neither light nor dark
then time and world return unsettled
a bed hastily remade

The Economy of the Celestial Empire

"I have always endeavored to acquire strict business habits; they are indispensable to everyone. If your trade is with the Celestial Empire, then some small counting-house on the coast, in some Salem harbor, will be fixture enough."

- Thoreau, at Walden

-----

sated and disengaging for sleep with the day on hold

settling into the spaces left unfilled

between recognized events and their relatives

that now seem drawn apart like the Red Sea

for something Other to pass through them

that likely passes through them daily unnoticed
as miracles not of rarity but recognition

as in a detective novel when the anti-hero
alternately stone-heart and bleeding heart
finds himself unsettled by a pause in the action
with killer and motive still not detected
the clues run down and out leaving only
disappointment, urgency and an emptiness
all too familiar, staring out the window of a motel
in a strange town looking at nothing, seeing nothing
when he notices a crow standing on the ground
beside a dumpster picking at a fast-food bag
reaching inside and taking out french fries
one at a time breaking them with its beak
and swallowing them fastidiously as if unfamiliar
with such fine dining being used to road-kill
it's dusty black feathers worn unevenly
she has neglected her grooming
when she turns to look his way her eyes are cold
assessing him as dinner and he wonders

if she sees something he hasn't yet noticed

if he has died in that room and has begun a slow awakening

beyond this life, the former one drifting like smoke

The News

seven billion souls

waves of data drench us

did we count the rats?

the news awaits us

Lazarus four days entombed

death leached of concepts

a crow lands on a fence

ten points achieved - exciting!

to count is to forget

in Bangladesh the rains

- to count is to remember -

delay until missed

on the home front costs
have long exceeded values
divorced, not speaking

four horseman parade
a fifth follows them naked
on a wooden horse

Plant Watch

many-handed like a home crowd welcomes a congressman
visiting his district with their petitions
a rhododendron supplicates the sun
with shiny hard-coated dark green leaves
each a pair of closed lips narrow at the corners

swollen in the middle each with the same

hard-to-read expression not quite a smirk

lips can't be expressionless even when asleep

but can be between expressions as these are

though even pauses can be read by intimates

the sun can be counted on most of the year

unlike politicians if you're asking and aren't paying

"Ahhhhh" they think and almost say

like the lips of sunbathers on a beach

in their paired and oiled hundreds a chorus

that would not have gathered singing but for sun

Ferrying

waddling away from one shore toward another

the big white boat lumbering, swaying

like a late-pregnant woman with a shopping cart

thickening the shining water with its mass
waves parting before and along it
with a lisp, a curl widening into another
untold movement in the indifferent Sound
before words began flowing out of it
unseen in the seeing, unheard in the hearing
the big diesels a distant hum of memory
a trembling felt through the decks
on other crossings, a churning below the waterline
white water boiling out behind us

freighted crossings like these define us
as those who know who we are
where we are and by intention soon to be
but by journeys made by the wisest of us ever
who left intending to but did not arrive
this crossing is both more and less productive

motion there is, and uniqueness, and levels of truth
some suitably described by words flowing from them
some experienced as indescribable, and these

allow the others to be truly known and to serve
as vessels carrying us slowly, slowly
into the indescribable unfreighted
experience of experience
our baggage sliding off the back of the boat
slipping away until there is only seeing of seeing

Paper Boats

your predecessor moved on to a much better position
on our recommendation (i.e., after a prolonged stay
in rehab was arrested for shoplifting and assault
and is now homeless in LA or Chicago or maybe Dallas)

no, I'm not seeing someone else (i.e., I sometimes
spend the night with two tattooed circus performers

of uncertain gender but only when I'm too drunk
to remember)

these investments while too difficult to explain
are nonetheless certified by an independent
accounting firm as rock-solid (AAA = most likely
to appeal to those who think slot machines
are investment instruments)

like crossing a swollen river in a paper boat
the wilder the river the thinner the newsprint
a few pages are all you'll need - guaranteed

truth is the afterlife of lies
    and their contagion:
heartache, lost savings, failed crossings
another job like a prison term
the liar's number and our own foolishness
and upon reflection not bitterness but a wiser innocence

Night Hunter

moonlight stains the night gun-barrel blue

windless, stale air sits over the city

above a tame lake ringed with manufactured light

an eagle floats, testing its newly enhanced

night vision from three hundred feet

on dozens of living fish swimming within

a foot of its surface, though not tonight

but as they did when this eagle

was a proud day-hunter, before a hurrying bus

struck it on a downward pass breaking its neck

now its eagle-life is in the currents

of the life of trees it rested on

of fishes and rodents it hunted

or watched and chose not to hunt

in the stillness and movement of air and water

held close by the great slow-turning earth

it remains to be imagined and presented
in currents of awareness inadequately known as time
that flow forward but can be discovered
to flow in any direction, to move without direction
to hold itself motionless gathering in
whatever can or could or did flow away from it

Self-Portrait

in a dark setting only the face is lit
as if from within - whatever else
might be there is unseen

the artist in triplicate
self, self as Other, and portrait

each as all and all as each

none of them look pleased
'not you again,' they're thinking
soon they'll be exploring the background

every work is self-portrait
most are much more as well, but here
all that is in the surrounding darkness

poor Rembrandt has another decade of life
a great artist enduring Learish misfortunes
he no doubt feels as enveloping darkness

every work is a self-portrait of the universe
a small boy gathers pine-cones in a park
each a miracle of prickly delight

Fox and Hare

Late afternoon of a New Year's Day 1856

a pleasant rumble from the Franklin stove

Thoreau at his table near a window

with notes from his daily walk, his journal

open to a clean page, a cup of tea

with a splash of home-made peach brandy

mostly for the candied summer scent

thinking of wide-spaced paw prints in snow

a foot deep near the railroad tracks

six and even seven feet of stride, a rabbit

in a hurry up a long slope at whose base

and then along the same path were footprints

alternating legs like foxes or dogs, then running

all-out but no match for the racing hare

whose prodigious leaps left great swathes

of snow unmarked on this remote stage

a drama with no witnesses HD imagines

the steel eyes of the fox, the timorous rabbit

its heart hammering in its white-furred chest

after a brief chase, a few seconds only, the fox accedes

and trots back down the hill, meanwhile HD

looking at the snow thinks of the long white body

of Miss Beatrice O'Rourke in whose father's tavern

he has spent some Boston nights listening

to her stories of her dear friend Emily Dickinson

who she said she closely resembled

after which they played fox and hare

upstairs in his room, though which is which

he can never decide or admit to

The next day's walk takes him back to the remote

section of railroad where the drama he imagined

seems different now, the rabbit running downhill

instead of uphill and the tracks he thought were fox

seem a practiced deception of a rabbit

maybe the same rabbit, inventing a solitary game

No Comet

At this hour the windows are unanimous

displays of the first of John of the Cross's three-in-one nights

the second held in reserve like a fresh battalion and the third

nearing discovery in its hidden flanking movement:

darkness of sense, of faith, and of God.

In a few minutes the trees will yawning stretch their branches

the bony limbs of an old apple tree and the prickly slights of pines

over the damp grass with its distressed fences pretending to recall

at least two visits of Halley's Comet and the last of the Mohicans.

The holly will raise its twist-faced leaves

each with a crown of spikes and its berries

noticing only red light. What wants seeing

needs our patient unknowing to bring its own light.

We wait bored in our camps a few sentries out

our new blue uniforms unbloodied

a stream of small game has been running through our camp

deer, possums, rabbits, raccoons - 'spooked by the sentries' -

but it is Jackson in the woods with his whole corps
his lines spreading out in assault formations
where there are no roads the clothing of his men
shredded by thickets and brambles.

July At-Bat

Fastballs low and inside, then low and just away
he almost swung at the second pitch, hands dropping
in a second from being cocked above his right
temple gripping the bat handle, its barrel hung
slightly below horizontal, to his right side
at the diaphragm, bat now vertical, halting
no call. Then a slider he swung through, bat whipping
in the zone with a low hum, his weight shifting right
to left. Step out, pop his spikes with the bat, settle

back in the box. Dead red middle of the plate musta
been ninety-five, swung late. Step out again, regroup
pitcher waiting, catcher waiting motionless, him on
the line now like a foot-long rainbow trout hook set
Step back in, reload. Pitcher winds, ball coming in

something off-speed outside maybe waiting waiting

late drop swooping over the back half of the plate

yakker Uncle Charlie rung-up growl of the ump

He turns walks away two of three times this season

A good year a career year high in the jet stream

decades pass in nine innings the very best of times

Absolute Christianity

1.

weathered hands plane boards for a table

but the mind is elsewhere, summering

in fields of light, in waves of light

roaring out over the desert

burning it clean and the hearts

of all its watchers then and now

"All the dazzling desirable things

of the known world I will give you as powers

for they are mine to give," says a familiar voice

with a slight lisp mocking its glibness,

"if you will give yourself to me."

Forty blistering days and nights pass

awaiting an answer. Remembered sheep graze

in meadows near a river, and in Lebanon

a measuring eye counts boards in living trees;

in markets the murmur of transactions

sealed with nods and money moving unceasing

hand to hand as if it were real

and not mere tokens for the day-long labor

of the poor who aren't in on the counting.

'I am not mine to give to the likes of you,'

says this watcher at last

this yet-to-be binder and liberator

of what flows through markets, meadows
pastures, woods, over outstretched seas
and embraces of men and women
an ignorance that speaks all tongues, a darkness
that would be light, a hope in deep disguise
as venality bound to the lisping prince:
'and what you own, you cannot give to me.'

2.

For the longest time he had no life, like the rest of us
disappearing between events memorable to some
but not others, and many who saw only a few of these
kept what they had grasped, raised moments
in which he all but vanished inside them, into what they heard
or saw and what it became in them
during their own disappearances between episodes
for we lack narrative unless and until someone constructs one
and he had promised them what they had never seen
nor heard, nor thought of, nor could imagine

the earliest narratives are lists of hearings, sightings

each with implied completeness

a timeless all-presence apparent to receptive readers:

a man born blind meets this odd travelling showman

develops inner sight and forgives his physical eyes their dysfunction,

a lame man meets him and discovers a marvelous current of intention

that needs no legs and rejoices,

a man harboring an inner cluster of demons meets him

and finds he can let them leave without losing himself also,

dead men hear, reconsider, return to life

a fig tree that grew up overnight to comfort Jonah

withers upon hearing from the minstrel it's metaphoric,

but a mustard seed hearing the same message

grows up overnight into a large bush to harbor

representative birds and a tree toad or two

3.

Great crowds of people come to the travelling show
sated on miracles, rumors, loaves and fishes
hear little of what the kindly fervent main man says
no one took notes, so what we begin with
are embodied memories, lived hearings
as he likely intended - and what hearings!
'The known human world is upside down, and we
will overturn it! A great reversal is upon us.'
'Virtue has become vice, and vice virtue.
Hidden truth withers. Proclaimed, performed
truth produces good out of evil as water from stones,
wine from water, manna from indifferent morning air,
as life from death - long slow transitions
because of our indifference.'

'blessed are those who know their own wickedness
for they may turn it into its opposite,
blessed are those who know their emptiness
for they may be filled,
blessed are they who can wait for justice
for they shall have it,

blessed are they who do not crave power
for the good they receive will not corrupt them,
blessed are those who learn to forgive
for they can receive forgiveness.'

4.

The travelling show broke up into pairs of minstrels,
and after the Original died they continued the practice
he found them called to, discouraging any cult of Himself
he had sent them out without provisions
as the Jehovah had sent Israel out of Egypt without provisions
to heal the sick, raise the dead, speak inarticulate truth into being
while the familiar world turned over like a gruff old lion
sleeping in the sun, not yet knowing what had become of it
in place of provisions they carry their hearings
'in the Great Reversal old allegiances will remain
only as transparencies neither dead nor living
except by a newly-risen Spirit
you and all you meet are become together
some in ignorance, some with knowledge

your task is to address the former as the latter
so that it may recognize itself and turn'

'these hearings become new in Others
divide their new owners into fierce oppositions
even among families, friends, communities formerly intimate
these truths need both acknowledgement and rejection
for neither can be without the other
as peace without war, love without hatred
good without evil'

5.

Centuries pass, not uneventful
hearings became a religion which returns
into its opposite, a cult of Himself
being easier than a wandering life
there are still only a handful of travellers
almost no one recognizes them now.
When the early texted hearings speak to us

they lie before us like Jonah spat out of a whale
half-dead on a beach, coughing, sputtering out phrases
recalled half-conscious without later reflections and re-workings
that have built up massively rigid like the Great Barrier Reef.
An anti-religion within a religion, these startled hearings
unexpected, out of nowhere, out of nothing
the ancients speaking to us, their history inverted into silence
the shaped silence of a concert hall without which
most of a performance is scattered unheard
unhearable, sound fallen among stones.
Not truths waiting to be heard, but just now forming
as heard, within the hearing, within the world of hearing
as the ongoing life of that world, as Absolute Christianity.

Hints of Sheridan Town

vigilance is the nature of the senses

and of the mind, can be turned

up or down but not off

dogs bark at a distance unseen

sunlight advances among the leaves

in an early July morning as birds

make their homing noises, puttering

and at a greater distance

an asynchronous ticking as in a clock shop

of sprinklers, dozens of them evenly spaced

along twelve-foot lengths of aluminum pipe

maybe five inches diameter, hitched to fireplugs

by great canvas-wrapped hoses

snaked out across the lawns like escaping organs

of a dying dragon, the hollow snap of the pipe

muted by water filling and passing through

in spurts somewhere between mechanical and organic

the lawns sparkling with their dew-like leavings
fifty years ago and now the sights and sounds
of morning settle as belonging together
as morning mind, mind of beginnings

Shark Bait

at night the sea was an old mad-woman clawing
at a body covered with boils, blind and thrashing
chanting tunelessly, vowels without consonants

a clean-swept morning came with a bit of psalm
remembered: 'come, listen, all who fear God...'
sunlight scanned them from an indistinct horizon

Casey held up a hand to shade her eyes, saw bones
glowing through it. Startled, she looked away. Later
in the same hooding gesture she couldn't see them

below in the small cabin Leonard made coffee,
eggs, bacon, toast with a fluid efficiency
she decided was his real nature, hard to fake

though his reticence was wearing on her, making
the trip seem longer than it was, a five-day jaunt
up the coast, for company just him and the sea

he watched the sea like a shepherd as though its sights
and sounds might slip away unnoticed, but he'd
favored her with Jameson, slow hands, endurance

when she had his full attention
  shorter than her by two inches
 he had dark eyes and taut weathered
skin and seemed to be watching for something sudden

was an Afghan war vet, wouldn't talk about it
startled awake at night to follow a small sound
had a store of secrets like rabbits in a bag

she was a gym rat, tall and plain and talkative
curious and uncommitted, she took photos
for a major news service when she had to work

the boat was a small sailor, thirty foot, almost
innocent but for a surprising large engine
that bellowed at full throttle like a charging tank

he said it belonged to an uncle when she asked
she'd done some summer sailing, helped him with the lines
sails shifting in the ancient art of wind-catching

using the engine was an anachronism
she'd caught the rhythms of older technology
the purposeful passivity of spreading sail

it was like relationships, where patience matters
while the Other learns his ego is a false guide
and there are older guides the heart and mind can trust

'why have I never been shy?' he wondered shyly

watching her from the stern as she sat on the bow
one leg on either side of the bowsprit, idle

in a frantic world with no known destination
watching birds answer the back-and-forth of small waves
with unthinking exaggeration in a less

resistant medium, her head moving side to side
in her body's medium he had thoroughly
explored yet had remained unknown to him unless

explored unknowing is a kind of knowledge
he sipped his coffee, she hers, the boat between them
the sails slack, a tiny current moving them on

he knew she wanted him to tell her something
of himself, something intimate. he considered
telling her of the survival imperative:

now as always, all you ever truly need
is to survive the next few minutes while the ultimate flow

of the world turns threats into opportunities

finishing his coffee he went back to reading
wind and water with an alertness begun as
practice become a peculiar paced involvement

2.

The attack came late the following afternoon
as under sail they passed a small island two grey
speedboats looped out at them ahead and behind,

coming fast, bows thrust up
 throwing out a wide white wake
their engines' song across the distance
 rising ominously as they approached

lashing the wheel
 Leonard yelled for Casey to get below

head-long dove into the cabin
came out with a long-barreled
rifle with scope and tripod
lay flat on the deck

sighted in on the nearest speedboat
fired three quick rounds
the boat spun away from them
out of course, slowed
as its wake lifted it
a body splashed into the water

Casey had seen snipers in Iraq, knew the hammering
clatter of assault rifles rising now from the boat
to starboard, saw Leonard turn to fire at them

struck repeatedly he crumpled, bloody, unmoving
and as wake from the pilotless speedboat raised them
slid overboard to port, still holding the rifle

and sank like a stone

knowing she had a few seconds
Casey rushed into the shallow cabin
grabbed her survival vest, strapped it on
came up low and dove overboard

in the direction Leonard had gone, swam hard for
the crippled speedboat, the vest slowing her, thinking
of a stack of small sealed drums in the bow locker

'survival rations' Leonard said when she found them,
not looking at her, but she'd been to the Afghan war
seen the poppy fields, heart of the real enemy

replacing hearts of dependent communities
with its ungoverned, implacable emptiness
the living death of a no-state a war can't save

no more than thirty yards from the boat now barely
moving, a splash in the water ahead of her
an explosion pounded her
stunned, face down, water

everywhere, no sound,

  limbs not responding, drifting

her legs sank, the vest pulled her head above water

cold, semi-conscious

  bits of her plan slid away

like Leonard's body

  no will, just bruised attention and memory

  survive the next few minutes

he had said, as you will no matter what you fear

death's a fear-construct

you power by believing,

can let go of

  doing so awakens something

invincible in you, something that turns destruction

aimed at you back at its ignorant carriers

a stun grenade, she thought

  they'll be coming for me

and I'm helpless
  a parade went by so slowly

she couldn't hear the band vigorously marching
cheeks puffed out pink on the wind-instramentalists
the drummers thumping soundless as out front, strutting

high-stepping, throwing her baton twenty feet up
spinning, flashing, then exploding into colored stars
and streamers, drifting lazily over the crowd

Casey recognized herself at last and struggled
to speak, couldn't, felt someone nudging her softly
in the back, felt a current carrying, dragging

her into a dark tunnel, the entrance fading
with the light, hearing only a distant high-pitched
whine like someone whistling her uncle's basement

3.

Waking took a long time, as she stood over her
motionless body, shaking its shoulders, calling
into its ears, lifting eye-lids, eyes unfocused

seeing itself vaguely then clearing in an odd
but familiar doubling, one ponderous as
the earth turning toward the sun, the other fluid

as sunlight pouring through a glass vase.   She lay still
in a small white room, its quiet space slowly becoming
her own - 'blessed is God, who has not withdrawn me

from his loving care,' she remembered, resolved
as the past week returned but not as it had been
a woman in a white dress entered with a clipboard

they talked; a Coast Guard chopper pilot picked her
out of the water near Homer AL - 'a small
drinking village with a fishing problem' - dolphins

had been seen pushing her toward the village, long beaked

common dolphins, eight foot, never seen this far north
the Coast Guard picked up a signal sent from her vest

its transmitter activated by the grenade
sent SOS and GPS, had memory
the FBI followed down the coast to the wreck

of Lenoard's 'uncle's' vessel lying beached, stripped
nearby two kill-shot bodies washed up bloated, chewed
and a metal canister of heroin marked 'flour'

Holbein's Dancers

("Since the springhead is timeless, its branches refresh.
Since neither can cease, what is the cause of your sorrow?'
- Rumi)

As cunning as a piper, Holbein's final visitor
gives its bones our horror for its costume
sometimes trailing remnants of winding-sheets
at others only giving hints of its lasting nakedness
through gaps in dress much like his customers
in some scenes the visitor comes as an Other
to drag away the living
but sometimes a closer read
shows Death an inner movement of the living
conferring with merchants, fighting with warriors
helping the plowman make long straight furrows

Montaigne lies motionless, stunned
thrown ten paces past his fallen horse
flying apart with their heels in the air
in a 16th-century civil war skirmish near his home
later he would feel the bruises
for now he feels only a drifting inwardness
with a nearly blissful current
leading under, outward, and away
as natural as sleep

he would lie there seeming dead for several hours
more truly, would lie there for the next 20 years
stirring now and then to think and write
from a near-death perspective, the negative movement
from one moment to another, a gathering-up appearing
as a leaving-behind that only much later
under close examination of thought and intuition
reveals itself as saving and renewing

not the fearful butchery religious fanatics
visited on whole villages of their opponents
as though they were vermin, not the vengeful destroyer
who makes his object nothing, but joyful dancers
who lead even these speechless moments
in a lively reel of renewal

'Death is of all things most dreadful
to hold fast requires the greatest strength;'
only tarrying with it do we see
its slow-emerging other face.

"My trade and art is living," Montaigne says

and Holbein's dancers are his fellows.

Scatterings

the late season's leaves
fallen on streets and sidewalks end up
mostly where motions leave them in gutters
against fences, in fields no one walks
no longer eye-and-mouth to trees
shedding themselves as larger layers of order
for a smaller chemical order

seeds have a different journey
template of a life broadcast profligate
of thousands one or two restart but of millions
forests are maintained and one can think of purpose
of failure and success unless blind

walking out through rows of taller corn

our Anti-Hero leads a few survivors away from the wreckage

an ordinary commuter flight between cities become

a flight he cannot leave, a manic survivor's glee

encapsulates him for many seasons he will not notice

hundreds or maybe thousands of slaves outcast

by an angry king outwitted by his better Self

now Occupy a Desert without water, meat or bread of slaves

where they find within themselves and on that barren land

the thirst of freedom and its answer

the hunger of freedom and its answer

and a deeper longing with no name and its answer

Forget the Apple

rounded and closed on itself, one shoulder
higher than the other and slumped
to one side, it has no edges
pale red with yellow highlights, bursting
with Vermeer light, as in the fruit bowl
in 'Girl Reading a Letter at an Open Window'
where several apples huddle with peaches
beaming back a bit of the golden flow
from the window, so full already
the yellow-white fruit inside all but visible
up close the surface is dotted with star-like points
strewn over it as if measured on a starry night
when distance obscures all but the nearest and brightest

but forget the apple, it knows nothing except
what I give it to be known as, stored like in a flash drive
a ruddy mirror of human mental processes

only by convention do you and I see the same apple
or either of us see it the same moment to moment

forget the apple embodying forgetfulness
em-bodying concepts briefly then slipping out of their embrace
lending itself to be thought
moment by moment then taking back
letting thought see its own no-body-ness
its lack of and dependence on bodies

she's forgotten the apples, the peaches
spilling out of a tipped bowl onto the bed
she's gone into a private space where the letter
has taken her, leaving us watching her not seeing
the brilliant-colored robes of the room of light

Vermeer: Girl Reading a Letter at an Open Window

Third Readers

maybe you read poems differently
after all it isn't like reading the news
intended for single use like kleenex
for me the first read is just for the music
of phrases and rhythm of lines
for the sounds of syllables nudging each other
half-serious provocations like children playing
the notes becoming or failing to become
a tune; if not I usually, but not always
turn the page, having so little waste-time
but for a tune I'll read again, this time
for emotions, their precursors
and successors, strident, longing
weary, welcoming, mushy, angry,
not naming but feeling them
and drawn to those I can't name
those yet to become familiar or refusing to
becoming something unique, requiring

a third reading where what's described

is just now happening, is only happening

on a third read and not just here and now

(whatever those mean) but as an arising

audience of third readers

have we understood? what's that?

we are a poem one of us has framed

Sherlock Holmes and the Mechanical T-Rex

Holmes sniffs. A Jules Verne fantasy
taken much too literally, chasing him
around a London warehouse in the
dead of night, its huge feet stomping
the stone floor with a grinding clatter
like mounted knight, smelling of grease
spouting diesel smoke from a belly-mounted
engine, its jaws steadily working rows
of sword-like teeth painted crimson

Watson lay still on the floor where the beast
had left him with a glancing blow
the Rex was surprisingly agile
driving Holmes toward and into a maze
of rooms and passages in the building's center

he began striding through the passages
following a scent, a current of fresh air
while behind him the monster, unable to fit
through the narrow walls, began
crushing them, battering them aside

a few minutes' careful observations, a few more
of reflection were all Holmes needed
there would be watchers above the maze
which had no ceiling, directing the beast
and there would be backup in case
he came out the other side, perhaps
a twin of the Rex behind him waiting its turn
at him, and Moriarty in a booth upstairs
with the beautiful, treacherous Urlaina
whose clever but not too clever lies
like her neckline suggested more by concealing less
leading him and Watson to this third act

Holmes wonders if Moriarty has discovered
an angel of light within himself, as he

had discovered his own inner contrarian
a terrifying dark angel whose true character
was usually masked by familiarity
who mocked Moriarty's designs as ambition
outrunning its means and mistaking
the form of its object, seeking preliminaries
when it should be seeking ultimates
not knowing good well enough to know evil

Forgiveness

is impossible. The plane waits
interminably at a loading dock while a crowd of pilgrims
with their gifts, greetings and promises of reformation,
their hopes and misdeeds, tickets and exchanges
boards for yet another unnecessary journey.
They have already arrived; forgiveness

isn't somewhere else, or anywhere

and yet it's here.

It lies on the ground in the early morning

beneath a fine mist, and we grope for it while half-awake,

our cherished discernment not yet powered up.

A young cynic finds it a small white disc and goes

in search of her laptop and MP3 while another finds it

a small feathered body like a bird with no wings

warm but with no heartbeat, and yet another

a disc-like tuning device, puts it to his lips

and it emits a low sound (or is it a high sound?) barely heard.

It sits in the last row of second class

an old woman in worn jeans and a baggy blue sweater

who might have been your mother, but when

you look again she's much younger in a fashionable coat

with a small child on her lap, and again

the child's alone this time, grown into a tall man with thick dark hair

and a penetrating look you cannot meet.

Gamma Ray Burst

four billion light-years away and here
in your mind, a star is ripped apart
by its galaxy's center, a giant black hole

with circumference a million kilometers
one side of the star that much closer
to the fierce gravity of a tightening cluster

of dead stars much stronger than
this star's own center-seeking
in a phenomenology of desire

the nearer side goes in first then draws
the rest after it, Ahab beckoning

dead from the back of the White Whale.

Desire recognizes itself in distances overcome

striding down a fairway in Augusta this April afternoon

a sleek pro-circuit stud ignores the crowd

stands a few feet behind the pleasingly white

dimpled ball and looks toward the green

and hundred and twenty yards, flag forward today

guarded by sand and water and a week's hard luck

pulling at him, dragging him off center, three strokes back

before he swings he sees the ball landing, bouncing, rolling toward the cup

The Known World's Edge

While clinging to the known world's edge

I spied a kinder place, where bees

hum Bach sonatas and the beasts

wear human face. A tall enchanted forest

gleams with tropical delights

the lion and the lamb exchange

identities at night

and visions answer questions muttered

underneath one's breath

or only dreamed, and denizens

no longer think of death.

Anticipation wearied me; I hustled back aboard

the ship of present state with its alternatives ignored.

This Walk

a sidewalk is built for walkers

conforms to street and houses, warms in the afternoon sun

an old American mule lumbers along it greying

to match the pavement, to fade into it

'show me, show me'

this walk not made for tourists shows us nothing

but for residents it leads to

the five marks of Suchness:

unique, peaceful, free of fixations

of concepts and of differentiation

it does have something to offer sojourners

am I walking when I begin or only after?

walking and I fade into each other

there is only the quiet street in August sunlight

not marked by footfalls it bears and doesn't hear

so neither do I when no longer a tourist

who has said too much already

Fire Life

theater in an iron box the flames devolve
each wooden audience into its elements
open a pale young flame of hope
in settled hearts - no more pity and fear please
let's stay with pleasantries

some logs burst out in passions in a tick
spending themselves all colors of fall leaves
Black Friday shoppers fighting over bargains
others glaciers chattering like Proust
a fine blue burning tells the others' names
that knew themselves only as an "I"
unsettled hearts - no more pity and fear please
let's stay with pleasantries

comedy will do or farce, or melodrama

let there be a little suffering of those
who've earned it like my neighbors
there; that's right. their bleeding serves an ache that others crave
at last, at last. a long reversal while all bleed
with blasted hearts - no more pity and fear please
let's back to pleasantries

all ashes now we tumble into sleep
the great resolve of theater leaves us whole when we awake
not quite remembering the passage of a dream
was I the quarterback? the mother with a baby on her lap?
the heart remembers fear and pity's pleas
as day resumes familiar pleasantries

204th Street

As our small top-down car hurls over it
for a moment the roadway writhes beneath us
like a nailed snake in a classic reversal
a head-stand moment of insight into motion-and-rest.
Then the road is again a shelf
between uphill and downhill slopes
both heavily wooded
a brilliant steely-blue sky peeks through a narrow overhead cut
and through airspace over downhill houses.
An unseen stream finds, keeps to low places
whose coolness has settled under the canopy
in early September and resists the late-summer heat.
As the little cars hums a windy passage
roars in our ears, a Now unmoved while moving
immediate, unfinished and over with
forever incomplete but longing to be

the double negation at the heart of time
making these as all memories
open, desperate invitations to all their descendants.

City-speak is not spoken here
a flutter-clatter of hurry immune to
the heady silence within all experience
several yet-mindless layers below our speed habit
if we were walking, or better still, if we were sitting
if we had learned to live in its ocean
we might be hearing it along with the necessary
unhearing, the double negation
at the heart of all truth that needs
our witness and then does not

The Autobiographies of Beau Tyler

1.

In a recurrent dream he drags a large fish across a beach
away from the water as if taking dinner home
a rope around its tail, its weight the most he can handle
leaning away from it his feet digging into the sand
now and then he stops to rest and notices
the water is no further away and the dune grass no nearer
sometimes the fish is a blue-gray shark with raptor teeth
exposed by lips pulled back in what might be a grin
its soulless eyes neither dead nor fully alive
its shutter-like gills opening once every five minutes or so

and closing with a muted slap,

occasionally it snorts as if stifling a laugh when Beau's back is turned.

He remembers it now as he watches urban landscape slide by

a window of a commuter train like magazine pages turning themselves

at the pace of a casual reader, wondering at the exotic links

between waking and dreaming that resist thought while provoking it.

A few run-down houses with battered cars and trucks parked on their lawns

small stores, large dirty multistory warehouses, workingman's taverns

all laced by blacktopped streets, ever-ready runways of the motor traffic

we need more space for than for any other human activity.

Cities are the traces of human activity; we are what we do primarily

and to see what's primary needs an ultimate discerning

like the double consciousness he calls 6E

(for experience, examining experience, examining examining experience) two turns: first from unreflected experience, then to seeing reflection

in which his very identity (an elusive but allegedly essential something)

and that of any object is put on indefinite hold

as when you're calling to report a power outage;

6E, a third inclusive reverie following the scent of truth down these streets and alleys

beginning with and then abandoning an illusion of improvisation.

2.

As an infant lying in a crib in the delirious pre-mind world

a rumble in his stomach indistinct from sunlight on pale orange walls

hunger from urgent thrashing of limbs, from a discontent become

a mewling, blubbering, wailing, screaming

relaxing into a nipple in the mouth the yeasty odor of milk

a chalky liquid warmly satisfying

linked now with an absent discontent in a peculiar

un-thought adversarial drama, one of many recurring

inventing time and space as their theatre

only later does it seem theatre is older than drama

and space-time older than either, waiting without purpose

an empty thought indifferent to their arrival and departure.

As a high-school football lineman he enjoyed the crash of helmets

shoulder-pads, spikes and knees, the grunting of young men hitting each other

with what they thought of as themselves: their uniformed

hormone-stoked young bodies, their collective frenzy, their intent

to inflict and to suffer injury in a semi-regulated brawl over icons

an inflated pigskin carried across line markers.

It was a sanctioned war game, one of many

remembered much later not as a narrative

but as isolated, unrelated moments

an elbow of a running back smashing into his chin

knocking his head back, his helmet off

but his size, momentum and beefy arms stop the runner.

Which game, which year this moment belongs to did not appear

as it no doubt had at the time, and he had come to accept

what appeared to him in this sort of reflection as truth;

he had not been there nor had the running back

nor had the men on both teams – at least not in 6E

and therefore maybe not at all.   After the second turn of reflection

he becomes this strange third seeing of transparencies and opacities.

As with a river there was flow but nothing that flows.

NoBo, the self he usually thought he was

listens with astonishment like Richard Nixon

learning it isn't true whatever a president does is legal.

'Don't give me this Buddhist crap,' he mutters

'I know who I am and I know what I know.'

There was more in this vein but no one was listening.

3.

As they hiked deeper into the woods

following an old footpath disappointingly well-used

this far from the city where wilderness

was somewhat less used than a city park

NoBo and Alice a sometime girlfriend

found the hills and trees repeating themselves

like passengers on a bus, cars on a freeway

the story behind the story was more of the same

but not to 6E in which there are no repetitions

a truth not apparent unless you notice uniqueness

arising not only from experience reflected on

but from the doubling of reflection, once and then again

by which all experience even memory is immediate.

Alice was leading and NoBo following watching her busy backside

when she turned suddenly and said: "You're so 6E."

"That's almost what I was just thinking about you," he replied

and they laughed, but it didn't happen: he'd imagined it

one of those intrusions he'd been learning to filter out.

With a nearer memory he could see the landscape repeating itself

then undo those repetitions with reflections

the untrained mind makes sameness of likeness for closure

as it tires of the endless novelty of experience

making a forest of Western redcedar and Douglas fir of a series of experiences

chaotically specific defying conceptualization except by brute force.

In much the same way a night at the symphony

unraveled by reflection began as a mental image of a magical music beast

shaped like a Chinese street dragon with trumpets and violins, cellos and basses

emerging from beneath its fluid-flexible red-and-gold skin

played awhile then replaced by kettle drums, pianos, oboes, French horns, clarinets

all sounded by the dragon, their voices all hers

a single orderly narrative pleasing and tonal

before the first turn of reflection the dragon played unseen

then briefly showed itself to NoBo's amazement

an imagining so juvenile at work within reception unrecognized,

immediate as the flutes and violins now seem

its unmasking leave suspicions of similar projections

at work in any perception of cymbals, violas, cellos

seemingly solid and enduring but concentration on them

dissolves tonality the notes now a cacophony

though this too become relations however negative

a flock of birds wheeling and sliding vaguely together in an autumn sky

herded by instinct and perception

the inner made outer and the outer inner.

You say south is this way? No, this way. No, this!

In a second reflective turn concepts no longer vanish when recognized

are slower to appear and no longer belong to an inner world

are no longer responses; inner and outer are now a single pane

of century-old window glass rippling erratically as it flows into the earth

like a memory losing details as it ages; these concepts endure, arising as objects

an outer clarity burning off like morning fog revealing an inner opacity

mysteriously unchanging, resisting the mind-eye's probing

but penetrable by the subtler play of intuition that is now seen

to product mind-stuff surrounding it like layers of atmosphere.

Hamlet. Blue Monk. The Magic Flute. Christine Falls. The Phenomenology.

A row of maples outside the window of his study he has given their names.

4.

Lying next to him Alice watches his eyelids flutter

the eyes moving beneath them probably chasing tail in another dimension

thinking for the hundredth time how he looks a bit like the Dude

in the Big Lebowski: beard, moustache, brown hair matted and tangled,

calling himself NoBo, a bit less verbal when asleep but not much

and given to slang that limits his audience to his generation's urban subculture

with a pot-head's detachment from everything except a moment's amusement

sometimes she thinks of herself as a joint he's down to the end of,

gripping it in a tiny clip, sucking the last whiff of pleasure out

before he discards it forgotten entirely

like every other man she's known

and yet when the genital madness passes he can be engaging

as long as one doesn't mistake it for commitment

like the other morning when he told her about the trees outside his window

each one has told him its secrets:

one's story he would dance out waving his arms overhead like a winded tree

humming what sounded vaguely like Classical Music

another had a long twisted story of a drunken pathologist and his sick family

told in what he described when asked as New Yorker voice

way too literate for NoBo unless she didn't really know him at all

another a crazy German epic with paragraph-long sentences

probing phenomena with the patient systematic intrusiveness of a colonoscopy

and another told in stately half-English a hundred years old at least

about a self-obsessed prince whose mother's horny for his uncle

Prince's father the king dies suspiciously while taking a nap in the garden

Prince's girlfriend drowns herself after he blows her off being crazy

there were other tree-tales but by now she'd decided

he'd been telling her he's just like Prince.

Thoreau Learns Pig-Catching

Henry David confides in us, his journal

on a soggy afternoon in early August 1856

he was already down the swollen river in his mind

paddling away from human sounds external and internal

gliding into the welcoming, open-hearted forest

seeing the season's flowers waiting for him

when his father told him the pig had jumped its fence

sometime after breakfast, and now the older man

looked to the younger to chase it down

HD suggested they sell the pig to a neighbor

at a discount, much like the private fire department

in ancient Rome would buy a burning house from its owner
drawing out the haggling while the building burned
but the elder Thoreau would not commit,
so the younger set out to learn pig-catching
a hundred pounds of pork, rind and all
muddy with cloven hooves and agile
with a few hours' lead, tasting unconfinement
could likely not be tempted by a pail of slops
this having failed before, and might have been long gone
but for lack of foresight and instincts dimmed by long captivity
HD saw the pig lying in the middle of the road
but when he approached, it upped and ran

through the long afternoon HD would find and lose the pig
several times, sometimes losing track of it for hours
'with swinish cunning and speed.....he is all ear and eye'
HD learns from his own pig-mind,
obstinate, hating confinement
but having no grasp of life unconfined
and waits for the pig to trap himself

meanwhile out on the river we who are now the journal
ride its current. listening to delta blues
mournful, despairing, obstinate and hating confinement
but self-confined, unwittingly conspiring with our captors
moving while watching and waiting for the fading
of these inner voices as woods, fields
wildflowers, deer, squirrels teach us the beginnings
of life beyond confinement

A Thousand Parodies

A hot-breath back-seat high-school girl forgot
herself (so she later claimed) in my old Ford
whose paint had once been ivory then faded
like old white linoleum, its plastic painted chrome
begun to bleed its color, seat-springs sagging,
engine hum accelerating like the muffled groan
of our coal furnace on a winter's day
hustling blanks the mind of consequences
they appear as if strangers
passing like the unwashed dead
not convinced of an afterlife but still hoping
to be relieved of a heaviness they cannot shed

love's revolution is known with and by its consequences
transparent, full of light
lacking those we stumble through

a thousand parodies until we find them,

join them formed up and waiting, a cast of thousands

waving, smiling, singing welcome from a vast plain

Workingman's Dreams

Hands and eyes moving in familiar patterns, he began

with rubber chickens tossed flat hand to hand

left to right belt-high then arched back eye-level right to left

two, then three, then four mustard-colored birds

with orange beaks and feet, bright red combs and shiny black eyes

that followed you if you watched them closely

which he couldn't do and keep the clumsy bastards airborne

humming "Uncle John's Band" for company

Kierney tried to grab the body of the birds but each catch

was unique, sometimes by necks or legs flung
spinning, making the return awkward. He'd learned to use
objects roughly the same size, shape and weight
for the unexpected release of daydreams arising
from rhythms of body and mind engaged
in nonsense seen as nonsense. It resembled his workday,
this insomnia-derived performance
in the garage with his box of well-worn props practicing
the dynamic balance of engagement
and detachment for dreaming. Once while dealing a Hummer,
the customer having caught the dreamed link
of ownership, a huge grey wolf muscled its way through
the office door widened in anticipation
wearing pink shades, a thick grey beard and a, well, wolfish grin
like Jerry shedding ownership in concert.

Upstairs asleep Nadine dreamed of cruising isles at Macy's
in lingerie when two buzzards flew in,
settled at the next display and explored the merchandise
"I'd stick with black," one muttered hoarsely.

As with Kierney and the dire wolf, she wondered who else
saw them, but so wondering caused the rest
to signal they were pretending not to. Dreams are public
but their shift-shapes evade waking notice
without a practice to negate the filters of desire
and belief. The chickens flew in circles.
A scrawny red pig in a bandanna climbed out
of the prop box playing raucous harmonica.

Death or Ice Cream

Will it be death or ice cream?

Miss Emily decides

while one is quickly melting

and the other long abides

a poem needs a subject either lingering or quick

the one the reader horrifies, the other makes her sick

intolerance of lactose had not yet been inferred

while other's joys in ice cream had long seemed to her absurd

but she is not her readers, and must regard their taste

or let her work in attic trunks be buried in disgrace

She grins. It must be tasty, making heart and stomach glow

for they choose its brief comforts over stations long and sure

the dead are ever who they were, but diners never know

if what went down so pleasant will survive the epicure.

A Hawk

Nothing human here but a thin boot trail

invisible a few yards off

a good hour's climb switchback up the ridge

Twenty years ago I set up my tent

in that clearing, back in the trees to avoid

damaging the frail meadow

the ground was stony under my sleeping bag

and thin carrying mattress

the light had sprinted off, and as it did

I noted what had brought me here wasn't here

And now? It could have been a hawk

floating high over the trees in the failing light

or not - I may have imagined it

Most clear, across the years is what was not there

an absence I brought with me and only now become visible

a hawk hunting its dinner, any dinner in near-darkness

www.ingramcontent.com/pod-product-compliance
Ingram Content Group UK Ltd.
Pitfield, Milton Keynes, MK11 3LW, UK
UKHW041925190726
13854UKWH00003B/1440